TITLE

Unveiling Al Nahyan: A Family Biography

Subtitle:

From Historical Roots to Modern Global Impact
\

BEN WHITE

Copyright © 2023 by Ben white

All rights reserved.

No part of this publication may be reproduced, distributed, or transmitted in any form or by any means, including photocopying, recording, or other electronic or mechanical methods, without the prior written permission of the publisher, except in the case of brief quotations embodied in critical reviews and certain other noncommercial uses permitted by copyright law.

Table of Contents:

Chapter 1. Introduction   6
    Defining Wealth and Legacy   6
    Significance of Family Fortunes   8

Chapter 2. House of Nahyan: From Bedouin Roots to Global Influence   11
    Early Origins in the Bani Yas Tribe   11
    Foundation of the Al Bu Falah Dynasty   13
    Abu Dhabi's Ascension: 18th Century to Present   14

Chapter 3. Leadership Saga: Rulers of Abu Dhabi   17
    Dhiyab bin Isa Al Nahyan: The Trailblazer   17
    Turbulent Times: Coups and Transformations   19
    Visionaries and Builders: Zayed bin Sultan and Khalifa bin Zayed   20

Chapter 4. Financial Powerhouse: Sovereign Wealth and Investments   23
    Al Nahyan's Stewardship: Abu Dhabi Investment Authority   24
    Mubadala Investment Company: A Global Player   25
    Managing Trillions: The Al Nahyan Wealth Empire   26

Chapter 5. The Al Nahyan Genealogy: Family Tree and Succession   29
    Charting the Lineage: From Dhiyab to Mohamed bin Zayed   29
    Shaping the Future: Mohamed bin Zayed's Leadership   33

Chapter 6. Controversies and Challenges   35
    Sheikh Issa bin Zayed: Scandal and Redemption   35

Inhumane Treatment: Princesses and Legal Battles 37

Chapter 7. Global Impact: The Al Nahyan Influence Beyond Borders **40**
Diplomacy and Alliances 40
Cultural and Philanthropic Contributions 42

Chapter 8. Legacy Beyond Wealth: Humanitarian Endeavors **45**
Education and Healthcare Initiatives 45
Preserving Cultural Heritage 48

Chapter 9. Comparative Analysis: The Al Nahyan Amongst the Elite **50**
Wealth Metrics and Rankings 50
Unique Features of Al Nahyan Wealth 52

Chapter 10. Future Outlook: The Next Generation **55**
Emerging Leaders within the Al Nahyan Dynasty 55
Evolving Investments and Strategies 56

Chapter 11. Conclusion **60**
Reflections on the Al Nahyan Legacy 60
Lessons from the Pinnacle of Global Wealth 62

Appendix **64**
Key Figures and Dates 64
A Glossary of Terms 65

Chapter 1. Introduction

- Defining Wealth and Legacy
- Significance of Family Fortunes

Defining Wealth and Legacy

Wealth is a complex and illusive term that goes beyond simple financial abundance. It also includes the richness of a family's intangible legacy, their influence, and the enduring legacy they leave on the world. When it comes to the richest families in the world, wealth is defined in a way that goes beyond traditional notions, taking into account things like material prosperity, cultural achievements, and the lasting legacy they leave behind.

Fundamentally, wealth is a dynamic force that changes along with the economic, social, and technological environments. Without a doubt, having financial success is important, but these families also have to manage a complex definition of wealth that takes into account the development and preservation of intellectual capital, cultural heritage, and a sense of civic duty in addition to material possessions.

The story gains a timeless quality from legacy's intertwinement with money. It is the lasting legacy these families leave behind, influencing philanthropy, industry, and government. The stories of legacy transcend the present and reverberate over successive generations, bearing witness to the vision, principles, and accomplishments of these distinguished families.

We explore the various interpretations of riches that have influenced these families' lives as we piece together the narratives underlying their prosperity. It is an enduring story that goes beyond balance sheets to examine the intangible assets that add to their societal stature.

Significance of Family Fortunes

Family wealth is significant in a way that is braided together by social duty, cultural influence, and economic influence. At the top of the global wealth pyramid, these families control whole sectors and economies by serving as guardians of vast riches and perpetuators of prosperity throughout generations.

In terms of wealth, these families' accumulations beyond conventional measurements. They develop into engines that spur entrepreneurship, stimulate innovation, and generate jobs globally. The economic significance goes beyond the establishment and maintenance of companies that frequently bear the family name and have a lasting impression on a variety of industries, including manufacturing, entertainment, and finance and technology.

Family wealth has evolved to be associated in culture with supporting and patronizing the arts, education, and charitable efforts. Frequently, these families found foundations, museums, and other cultural establishments that grow into strongholds of innovation, learning, and advancement in society. The contributions of these families, who use their money to support cultural expression and conserve legacy, improve the humanities, sciences, and arts.

The significance of family riches takes on an intrinsic social obligation. These families control a great deal of social and environmental policy because they are guardians of substantial wealth. Their charitable activities target global issues, such as environmental sustainability, healthcare, and education, and they have a real and beneficial influence on communities all over the world.

We disentangle the complex relationship between wealth and social advancement by examining the role of family fortunes. These families end up being change agents who influence national policies and advance human welfare. A fascinating story that captures the essence of belonging to one of the wealthiest families in the world is formed by examining their positions in the social, cultural, and economic realms.

In order to uncover the many facets of wealth and legacy that define the narratives of these remarkable families, we will be peeling back the financial success layers as we undertake our investigation. A new aspect of their lives is revealed in each chapter, highlighting how intricate and intertwined their fortunes are and how much of an impact they have on the global scene.

Chapter 2. House of Nahyan: From Bedouin Roots to Global Influence

- Early Origins in the Bani Yas Tribe
- Foundation of the Al Bu Falah Dynasty
- Abu Dhabi's Ascension: 18th Century to Present

A fascinating story spanning centuries, from modest Bedouin beginnings to the height of world prominence, is told through the House of Nahyan's chronicle. Steeped in the Bani Yas Tribe, this distinguished family has not only seen Abu Dhabi undergo tremendous change, but they have also played a pivotal role in the city's rise to prominence globally.

Early Origins in the Bani Yas Tribe

The Bani Yas Tribe, a Bedouin nomadic group, wandered the vast deserts where the House of

Nahyan had its start. The trip that the Bani Yas undertook in the 18th century, under the visionary leadership of Dhiyab bin Isa Al Nahyan, would change the course of history. When the Bani Yas arrived on the barren dunes of Liwa Oasis, a legacy that would ultimately determine Abu Dhabi's fate began.

A dynasty that would last for generations was established by the charismatic leader and founder of the Al Bu Falah Dynasty, Dhiyab bin Isa Al Nahyan. Because of their strong tribal ties, the Bani Yas served as the foundation for the legacy that the House of Nahyan would leave behind. The hard desert climate of those early years shaped a people with a strong bond with their homeland and an unwavering determination that would guide them in all of their future pursuits.

Foundation of the Al Bu Falah Dynasty

Under the reign of Dhiyab bin Isa, the House of Nahyan, a branch of the Bani Yas Tribe that originated from Al Falahi, saw its foundations cement. Dhiyab bin Isa Al Nahyan established the Al Bu Falah Dynasty, which would eventually become the royal family of Abu Dhabi, while serving as the head of the Bani Yas tribal confederation.

An important turning point in Abu Dhabi's history was the creation of the Al Bu Falah Dynasty. Beyond tribal affinities, the dynasty consolidated authority and established the foundation for the emirate's future significance. The foundation for the House of Nahyan's long-lasting influence was laid by the leadership, governance, and strong devotion to the welfare of the populace that characterized the Al Bu Falah heritage.

Abu Dhabi's Ascension: 18th Century to Present

The story of the House of Nahyan is akin to Abu Dhabi's ascent from a sleepy seaside hamlet to a major world power. Ever since taking over in 1793, the Al Nahyan family has played a crucial role in determining the course of the emirate. The visionary leadership of the Al Nahyan rulers is inextricably tied to Abu Dhabi's transformation from a regional outpost to a booming city.

Under the leadership of the Al Nahyan family, Abu Dhabi began to change in the eighteenth century. The ruling class promoted stability and prosperity while navigating the difficulties of the day. After settling in Abu Dhabi, the Bani Yas rose to prominence as the ruling class, steering the emirate through several periods of transition.

The renovation of Abu Dhabi was made possible in large part by the efforts of Zayed bin Khalifa

Al Nahyan in the late 19th and early 20th century. His leadership and vision made it possible for other monarchs to carry on the heritage. After oil was discovered in the middle of the 20th century, Abu Dhabi gained even more international recognition. The House of Nahyan took advantage of this newfound economic power and made investments in the emirate's infrastructure, healthcare system, and educational system.

In 1971, the United Arab Emirates was founded and its first President was Zayed bin Sultan Al Nahyan, a prominent member of the family. Abu Dhabi became a major role in regional and international affairs as a result of his statesmanship and dedication to progressive policies.

Khalifa bin Zayed Al Nahyan, the second President of the United Arab Emirates, carried on the legacy by helping the nation navigate the difficulties of the twenty-first century. During his administration, strategic investments and a dedication to sustainable development saw Abu Dhabi's rise to prominence as a worldwide financial centre.

The organization's current leader, Mohamed bin Zayed Al Nahyan, exemplifies a contemporary, visionary management approach. As the UAE's current president, he has the ability to further mold Abu Dhabi's standing in the world by means of bold plans, astute investments, and a dedication to economic diversification.

From the barren deserts of the Bani Yas Tribe to the bustling metropolis of contemporary Abu Dhabi, the House of Nahyan's journey is a monument to their tenacity, innovative leadership, and dedication to a legacy that lasts for centuries. This extraordinary family's impact is felt well beyond the emirate's boundaries, having a lasting impact on both the history of the United Arab Emirates and the international scene.

Chapter 3. Leadership Saga: Rulers of Abu Dhabi

- Dhiyab bin Isa Al Nahyan: The Trailblazer
- Turbulent Times: Coups and Transformations
- Visionaries and Builders: Zayed bin Sultan and Khalifa bin Zayed

The Al Nahyan family, a lineage of rulers who successfully navigated through difficult times and pivotal stages to emerge as visionaries and builders of a nation, is deeply ingrained in Abu Dhabi's history. The narratives of important individuals in this leadership story are told, and each one leaves a lasting impression on the course of the emirate.

Dhiyab bin Isa Al Nahyan: The Trailblazer

Dhiyab bin Isa Al Nahyan, a pathfinder whose vision and leadership created the groundwork for the enduring rule of the Al Bu Falah Dynasty, stands at the origin of the Al Nahyan tradition. Dhiyab bin Isa became a prominent leader during the period when the Bani Yas Tribe roamed the parched terrain of Liwa Oasis.

After Dhiyab bin Isa Al Nahyan took over as king in 1761, Abu Dhabi became its first sovereign. The endurance and togetherness of the Bedouin people were reflected in his style of leadership. Dhiyab, the founder of the Al Bu Falah Dynasty, created a system of government that prioritized tribal unity and set the stage for the family's long-lasting dominance.

But a power struggle within the family brought to his downfall in 1793, and his rule was beset by internal problems. Nevertheless, Dhiyab's reputation persisted because of his position as the trailblazer who put Abu Dhabi on the path to independence and regional prominence.

Turbulent Times: Coups and Transformations

The eras that the succeeding rulers ruled over were characterized by internal conflict, coups, and outside influences. The successor to Dhiyab, Shakhbut bin Dhiyab Al Nahyan, faced difficulties from 1793 to 1816. Under his leadership, the balance of power shifted, and in 1816 his own son, Muhammad bin Shakhbut Al Nahyan, eventually deposed him.

Muhammad's rule was short-lived, though, since Tahnun bin Shakhbut Al Nahyan, his brother, overthrew him with his father's help. A number of internal conflicts emerged at this time, which was indicative of the difficulties associated with changing leadership within the Al Nahyan family.

Unrest also characterized Tahnun bin Shakhbut's reign, which finally resulted in his death in

1833. Over the next few decades, a number of rulers faced coup attempts, and the political climate in Abu Dhabi was significantly shaped by the internal dynamics of the Al Nahyan family.

An important turning point came with Zayed bin Khalifa Al Nahyan's succession in 1855. Under his direction, there was some stability, and the conditions were met for Abu Dhabi to become a major player in the area. The emirate's future wealth was made possible by the peace and progress that marked Zayed's tenure.

Visionaries and Builders: Zayed bin Sultan and Khalifa bin Zayed

Abu Dhabi was converted into a modern, vibrant nation by the visionary and builder Zayed bin Sultan Al Nahyan and Khalifa bin Zayed Al Nahyan, two powerful leaders in the Al Nahyan lineage.

Born in 1918, Zayed bin Sultan assumed the presidency of the United Arab Emirates in 1971 after a series of calculated political manoeuvres. His leadership, which was widely regarded as inclusive and smart, was crucial to the establishment of the United Arab Emirates. Zayed envisioned a unified federation that would utilize its emirates' combined strength.

The discovery of oil was the main driver of Abu Dhabi's extraordinary economic growth during Zayed's leadership. From a little coastal town, the emirate developed into a major player in the world with a diverse economy. Modern Abu Dhabi was made possible by Zayed's dedication to social welfare, education, and infrastructure development.

In 2004, Zayed's eldest son, Khalifa bin Zayed Al Nahyan, took over as President of the United Arab Emirates. Under his direction, the tradition of advancement and stability was upheld. Under Khalifa's leadership, Abu Dhabi strengthened its standing as a major international financial center. His administration was marked by strategic investments, sustainable development initiatives, and a concentration on healthcare and education.

This visionary leadership is being carried out by Mohamed bin Zayed Al Nahyan, the current head of the Al Nahyan family and President of the United Arab Emirates. His calculated moves, such as projects aimed at sustainable development and economic diversification, highlight the family's dedication to guaranteeing Abu Dhabi's continued prominence in international affairs.

The Al Nahyan family's leadership story is one of tenacity, foresight, and metamorphosis. Every emirate's future has been shaped differently by each of its rulers, from the modern Abu Dhabi to the dry deserts of the Bani Yas Tribe. As long as the House of Nahyan stands as a symbol of stability and advancement in the United Arab Emirates, the leadership heritage will endure.

Chapter 4. Financial Powerhouse: Sovereign Wealth and Investments

- Al Nahyan's Stewardship: Abu Dhabi Investment Authority
- Mubadala Investment Company: A Global Player
- Managing Trillions: The Al Nahyan Wealth Empire

The Al Nahyan family is incredibly wealthy, and their wealth goes far beyond conventional leadership. The Abu Dhabi Investment Authority (ADIA) and Mubadala Investment Company, two important organizations that have a significant impact on the global financial scene, are at the center of their influence. They oversee an empire of sovereign wealth that is meticulously maintained.

Al Nahyan's Stewardship: Abu Dhabi Investment Authority

The Al Nahyan family's wise management of financial resources is demonstrated by the Abu Dhabi Investment Authority (ADIA). ADIA was one of the biggest sovereign wealth funds in the world when it was founded in 1976 and gained popularity fast. ADIA has grown to be a key component of Abu Dhabi's economic plan under the direction of the Al Nahyan administration.

Infrastructure, real estate, fixed income, and stocks are just a few of the many industries included in ADIA's investment portfolio. The fund has made a substantial contribution to Abu Dhabi's long-term financial sustainability thanks to its cautious but strategic approach to investing, which has helped it weather global economic turbulence.

The Al Nahyan family's devotion to caution and foresight is seen in their leadership in creating ADIA's investment plans. ADIA's capacity to handle the intricacies of international markets has allowed them to act as a stabilizing influence during periods of economic turbulence, bolstering Abu Dhabi's standing internationally.

Mubadala Investment Company: A Global Player

Another cornerstone of the Al Nahyan family's financial empire, the Mubadala Investment Company, complements ADIA's function. With the goal of promoting economic diversification for the Emirate of Abu Dhabi, Mubadala was founded in 2002 and functions as a worldwide investment and development firm.

The portfolio of Mubadala is distinguished by its strategic investments in industries like technology, healthcare, energy, and aerospace. With a presence in several important markets throughout the world, the company not only helps Abu Dhabi diversify its economy but also promotes cooperation and partnerships across borders.

The foundation of the Al Nahyan family's plan for Mubadala is building a vibrant, internationally competitive organization. Through the utilization of Mubadala's skills, the family has been instrumental in establishing Abu Dhabi as a center for innovation, technical progress, and sustainable development.

Managing Trillions: The Al Nahyan Wealth Empire

The enormous fortune managed by ADIA and Mubadala highlights the Al Nahyan family's financial power. They are among the most powerful financial organizations in the world, with combined assets under control estimated to be in the trillions of dollars.

A deep grasp of geopolitical dynamics and global economic trends is necessary for the careful administration of such substantial wealth, in addition to financial acumen. Maintaining and expanding their financial empire has been made possible by the Al Nahyan family's dedication to diversification, risk management, and long-term sustainability.

The Al Nahyan financial empire is significant in ways that go beyond personal wealth. Their investments have had a profound effect on the development of Abu Dhabi's economy, encouraging creativity, and helping the emirate become a major player in the world economy.

Ultimately, the financial behemoth the Al Nahyan family built with the Abu Dhabi Investment Authority and Mubadala Investment Company is proof of their strategic foresight and dedication to Abu Dhabi's economic development. The Al Nahyan family has enormous global influence due to their role as custodians of trillions of dollars' worth of assets. They have demonstrated their ability to successfully negotiate the intricate world of international finance while refusing to lose sight of their emirate's sustainable growth.

Chapter 5. The Al Nahyan Genealogy: Family Tree and Succession

- Charting the Lineage: From Dhiyab to Mohamed bin Zayed
- Shaping the Future: Mohamed bin Zayed's Leadership

Charting the Lineage: From Dhiyab to Mohamed bin Zayed

Tracing its heritage back to the Bani Yas tribe, the Al Nahyan family's origins are deeply ingrained in Bedouin tradition. Dhiyab bin Isa Al Nahyan, the pioneer who established the Al Bu Falah dynasty in 1761, is at the head of this illustrious family tree. Under his guidance, the family started to gain prominence in the area and left a legacy that lasted for generations.

Al Bu Falah dynasty, which now governs Abu Dhabi, was established as a result of the leadership of Dhiyab bin Isa Al Nahyan as the head of the Bani Yas tribal confederation. His tactical acumen and adept handling of the historical obstacles paved the way for later generations to mold the course of the Emirate of Abu Dhabi.

Key personalities appear as the family tree branches out, each adding to the rich fabric of Al Nahyan history. Following in his father's footsteps, Shakhbut bin Dhiyab Al Nahyan led the family during a time of stability and expansion. The complicated process of succession persisted, and the family's history was profoundly impacted by prominent individuals like Tahnun bin Shakhbut Al Nahyan and Zayed bin Khalifa Al Nahyan.

The story of the family revolved around Zayed bin Khalifa Al Nahyan, who was born in 1835. During his reign, Abu Dhabi became a major regional player, which was an important chapter in the city's history. Being the grandfather of Sheikh Zayed bin Sultan Al Nahyan, the man responsible for the establishment of the United Arab Emirates, Zayed ibn Khalifa's influence continues long after his death.

Succession Planning and Tahnoun bin Zayed bin Khalifa Al Nahyan

The Al Nahyan family's succession is a well planned procedure that is informed by both tradition and modernity. Tahnoun bin Zayed bin Khalifa Al Nahyan, who took over as leader in the early 1900s and led Abu Dhabi through a period of profound change, was born in 1857. His dedication to the emirate's welfare and the family's ideals set the stage for later leaders.

Sultan bin Zayed bin Khalifa Al Nahyan and Hamdan bin Zayed bin Khalifa Al Nahyan carried on the family tradition and added to the story of Abu Dhabi as it developed. But as the fratricide between Hamdan and Sultan shows, internal dynamics can occasionally have unfavorable results, highlighting the complexity of leadership.

The story of leadership continues with 1918-born thinker and builder Zayed bin Sultan Al Nahyan. The United Arab Emirates were founded in 1971 as a result of the revolution sparked by his rise to power in 1966. Being the first President of the United Arab Emirates embodies Zayed bin Sultan's lasting influence on the country's progress.

In 2004, Zayed bin Sultan's son Khalifa bin Zayed Al Nahyan replaced his father. The Al Nahyan family's dominant position in the UAE's government was cemented during his nearly two-decade rule, which ended in 2022. Modernization, economic diversification, and regional stability were priorities during Khalifa bin Zayed's leadership.

Shaping the Future: Mohamed bin Zayed's Leadership

The leadership of Mohamed bin Zayed Al Nahyan denotes the modern era in the Al Nahyan family's history. Born on March 11, 1961, Mohamed bin Zayed became the Crown Prince of Abu Dhabi in 2004 and the President of the United Arab Emirates in 2022.

In order to keep Abu Dhabi moving forward into a dynamic future, Mohamed bin Zayed's leadership style strikes a balance. His focus on innovation, sustainable development, and international collaborations highlights the family's dedication to adjusting to the demands of the twenty-first century.

The Al Nahyan family continues to be crucial in determining the future of Abu Dhabi and the United Arab Emirates under Mohamed bin Zayed's leadership. The family's long-lasting dedication to the welfare and prosperity of the emirate is demonstrated by the complex genealogy that has been weaved over centuries of leadership. With the vision of Mohamed bin Zayed guiding them, the Al Nahyan family tree is poised to grow and leave an enduring legacy that will be recorded in history.

Chapter 6. Controversies and Challenges

- Sheikh Issa bin Zayed: Scandal and Redemption
- Inhumane Treatment: Princesses and Legal Battles

Sheikh Issa bin Zayed: Scandal and Redemption

Even though the story of the Al Nahyan family is remarkable in many ways, disagreements have arisen over it. A prominent incident involving Sheikh Issa bin Zayed, a member of the royal family, garnered global attention and prompted discussions about justice and accountability.

A scandal involving Sheikh Issa in April 2009 revealed horrifying cases of torture and abuse. A video purportedly showing Sheikh Issa ruthlessly torturing a victim appeared online. The disclosure shocked the world and made people wonder if influential people, even those from royal families, were really accountable for their actions.

Concerns over the internal dynamics and checks and balances within the Al Nahyan family were also raised by the incident, which brought attention to human rights issues. A complicated interaction between established hierarchies and the demand for accountability in a contemporary, globalized society was set off by Sheikh Issa's deeds.

Following the uproar, efforts were made to limit the damage and make amends. The Al Nahyan family's task was to respond to the accusations and lessen the harm to their image. It highlighted the tightrope royal families had to walk in order to preserve their historical power while also adjusting to changing social norms.

Inhumane Treatment: Princesses and Legal Battles

The Al Nahyan family encountered difficulties that went beyond the acts of a single member and included more general problems with the dynamics of the family. Several Emirati princesses from the Al Nahyan family became embroiled in a judicial dispute in 2017 that exposed mistreatment of domestic workers.

A Belgian court declared that many princesses were responsible for the cruel treatment of their attendants during events that took place in 2007 and 2008. Human rights concerns were raised by the ruling, including the way that disadvantaged people are treated in wealthy houses.

The court proceedings underscored the need for accountability, irrespective of social standing, and revealed the difficulties in upholding privacy and customs within royal families.

Renowned for their wealth and power, the Al Nahyan family was forced to negotiate a challenging environment where family obligations and legal requirements collided.

Regarding the place of royal families in modern society, the debates surrounding the examples of cruel treatment brought up more general issues. The expectations of transparency and respect to universal ethical norms were placed against the traditional concepts of privilege and authority.

In order to overcome these obstacles, the Al Nahyan family had to face internal conflicts, reexamine procedures, and negotiate the nuances of legal responsibility. The court cases acted as a reminder that a person's activities within a royal family can have far-reaching effects that transcend national boundaries in today's globalized world.

To conclude, the disputes and difficulties encountered by the Al Nahyan family offer a complex viewpoint on the meeting point of custom and innovation. As royal families struggle with shifting social norms and increased public scrutiny, these episodes highlight the necessity for flexibility and accountability among their ranks. In light of the obligations that come with their prominent position in the world, the Al Nahyan family's response to these difficulties illustrates the careful balance they must achieve to maintain their legacy.

Chapter 7. Global Impact: The Al Nahyan Influence Beyond Borders

- Diplomacy and Alliances
- Cultural and Philanthropic Contributions

Diplomacy and Alliances

With strategic alliances and diplomacy, the United Arab Emirates (UAE), home to the House of Nahyan, has had a significant worldwide influence. The current head of the family and President of the United Arab Emirates, Sheikh Mohamed bin Zayed Al Nahyan, is in the forefront of this influence. The Al Nahyan family is now recognized as major figures in the shaping of geopolitical environments thanks to his imaginative approach to international interactions.

Al Nahyan's diplomatic approach has placed a great emphasis on forming ties with countries all over the world. Under his direction, the UAE has become known as a trustworthy and powerful ally in a number of global endeavors. Beyond just economic cooperation, this diplomatic outreach touches on issues like security, technology, and healthcare.

Global diplomacy now centers around Abu Dhabi, the capital of the United Arab Emirates and home to the Al Nahyan family. In a geopolitical landscape that is always shifting, the family's leadership has been essential in settling disputes within the area, supporting peace initiatives, and promoting stability. The influence of the Al Nahyans extends beyond the boundaries of the United Arab Emirates and is felt at global fora where choices affect the destiny of entire countries.

The family maintains diplomatic ties to rising economies, regional organizations, and powerful nations. The foundation of these alliances is a long-term global cooperative vision that goes beyond short-term gains. The Al Nahyan family's dedication to diplomacy is a reflection of their awareness of how intertwined all countries are and how important it is to work together to overcome common problems.

Cultural and Philanthropic Contributions

The Al Nahyan family has significantly influenced international culture and philanthropy outside of the spheres of politics and diplomacy. Cross-border initiatives demonstrate their dedication to protecting and advancing cultural heritage.

World-class museums, art exhibitions, and educational programs can be found in Abu Dhabi, which has become a cultural hub under the Al Nahyan family's leadership. In addition to supporting the arts, the family collaborates with well-known worldwide organizations to promote intercultural understanding and dialogue.

The cornerstone of the Al Nahyan heritage is philanthropy, including programs involving worldwide healthcare, education, and humanitarian help. From reducing poverty to improving access to healthcare, the family's charitable institutions have been instrumental in tackling important concerns. A larger goal of enhancing human welfare is in line with this dedication to social responsibility.

The Al Nahyan family has a profound confidence in the ability of compassion and culture to transcend boundaries, which is shown in their influence in the cultural and humanitarian sectors. This philosophy goes beyond simple financial contributions. The family helps create a more cohesive and interconnected world by sponsoring programs that advance diversity, tolerance, and education.

In summary, the Al Nahyan family's influence is felt far beyond the UAE's boundaries. The family has established itself as a major force on the international scene by deft diplomacy, calculated alliances, and significant cultural and charitable donations. The Al Nahyan effect is evidence of royal families' ability to favorably impact world affairs by promoting understanding and cooperation in a world growing more interconnected by the day.

Chapter 8. Legacy Beyond Wealth: Humanitarian Endeavors

- Education and Healthcare Initiatives
- Preserving Cultural Heritage

Education and Healthcare Initiatives

Presumably powerful and affluent, the Al Nahyan family has left a lasting legacy that goes well beyond material success. Fundamental to their influence is a strong dedication to humanitarian projects, especially those related to healthcare and education. The family's commitment to these causes shows that they have a deep appreciation for the ability of knowledge to improve lives and the value of readily available healthcare in creating societies that are resilient.

The Al Nahyan family's charitable endeavors have always revolved around education. They have led efforts to improve educational opportunities both in the UAE and around the world because they understand the critical role education plays in defining the future. The family has worked to provide people with the means to make significant contributions to society through partnerships with academic institutions, educational initiatives, and scholarships.

The Al Nahyan family's impact on education is evident throughout the United Arab Emirates. Their dedication to promoting a knowledge-based society is demonstrated by the creation of top-tier research institutes, universities, and educational institutions. The family's encouragement of worldwide education projects has allowed students from various backgrounds to take advantage of educational possibilities that might not have been available to them otherwise, extending beyond national boundaries.

The Al Nahyan family's humanitarian activities also center on healthcare. Their dedication to enhancing healthcare infrastructure and accessibility is demonstrated by the creation of cutting-edge medical facilities and programs designed to address urgent health issues. This includes spending on health research, preventing illness, and improving healthcare systems—not just in the United Arab Emirates but also in other areas where there are health inequalities.

The family's healthcare endeavors go beyond physical establishments. They have been crucial in aiding international health campaigns, advancing health education, and fighting infectious diseases. Through the utilization of their wealth and power, the Al Nahyan family has contributed to the advancement of the global health agenda, coordinating with larger initiatives to guarantee health parity for all.

Preserving Cultural Heritage

The preservation of cultural heritage bears witness to the Al Nahyan family's appreciation of identity and the diversity of human history. The family has actively supported philanthropic efforts to protect and promote cultural heritage both domestically in the United Arab Emirates and internationally.

The establishment of museums, cultural institutions, and historical celebration projects around the United Arab Emirates is indicative of the family's dedication to maintaining the country's cultural legacy. To ensure that future generations have a strong connection to their roots, this involves the preservation of cultural practices, traditional arts, and archaeological sites.

The Al Nahyan family has supported initiatives around the world that work to preserve and advance cultural diversity. Their efforts to preserve historical sites, relics, and customs have crossed national boundaries and promoted a feeling of common human heritage. The family adds to the global fabric of variety and understanding by funding programs that promote cultural identity.

In summary, the Al Nahyan family's legacy is intricately linked to their dedication to humanitarian causes and extends beyond their financial success. By making well-timed investments in healthcare, education, and cultural heritage preservation, the family has permanently impacted society. Their legacy encourages other powerful families to use their fortune for the benefit of humanity, understanding that genuine wealth is found in one's ability to positively influence other people's lives as much as material possessions.

Chapter 9. Comparative Analysis: The Al Nahyan Amongst the Elite

- Wealth Metrics and Rankings
- Unique Features of Al Nahyan Wealth

Wealth Metrics and Rankings

Families everywhere are accumulating fortunes of differing sizes, creating a diverse global wealth landscape. Not only in the Middle East but also internationally, the Al Nahyan family is a prominent force among the elite. A detailed examination of important indicators and their relative wealth to other wealthy families is necessary to comprehend their wealth.

A family's net worth is one indicator that's frequently used to assess their financial situation.

Due to their extensive resources, which include investments, sovereign wealth funds, and oil revenues, the Al Nahyan family has amassed a considerable amount of wealth. To gauge the extent of their financial sway, one can compare their net worth to that of other wealthy households. Our examination of global wealth rankings takes into account various elements, including investments, assets, and overall financial impact.

Comparative analysis also emphasizes the importance of wealth source diversification. The Al Nahyan family's riches is inextricably linked to their strategic holdings in the Abu Dhabi Investment Authority and Mubadala Investment Company, in contrast to other wealthy families who depend on particular business fields or industries. Examining the wealth portfolio's diversification reveals how resilient the family has been in the face of changing global market conditions and economic ups and downs.

Unique Features of Al Nahyan Wealth

What makes the wealth of the Al Nahyan family unique from other wealthy families is its unique feature. The tactical administration of sovereign wealth funds is one such characteristic. Their stewardship has allowed the Abu Dhabi Investment Authority to grow into one of the world's biggest sovereign wealth funds. Examining the distinct approaches utilized in the administration of these assets offers valuable perspectives on the family's financial know-how and future outlook.

With holdings in a variety of industries, such as infrastructure, technology, and energy, the family's power also transcends conventional sectors. A closer look at the industries in which the Al Nahyan family has made sizable investments reveals their methodical approach to making money. Through diversification, the family is positioned to play a significant role in influencing global economic trends while also reducing risks.

An additional characteristic of the Al Nahyan family's wealth is their dedication to philanthropy. A qualitative element is added to the family's legacy by their contributions to cultural preservation and humanitarian causes, even though financial success is frequently quantified in nominal terms. It is evident how different wealth can be used to advance society when comparing this family's philanthropic endeavors to those of other wealthy ones.

The Al Nahyan family's wealth can be better understood by comparing them to other members of the global elite and taking into account both their distinct characteristics and net worth metrics. Comprehending their place within the global wealth hierarchy offers important perspectives on the workings of family wealth and the complex ways in which their influence is felt worldwide.

Chapter 10. Future Outlook: The Next Generation

- Emerging Leaders within the Al Nahyan Dynasty
- Evolving Investments and Strategies

Emerging Leaders within the Al Nahyan Dynasty

Focus shifts to the young dynasty leaders who could influence the Al Nahyan family's course in the twenty-first century. Understanding the people who will continue the legacy gives insight into the family's continuity, and the leadership transition is a significant event. This section delves into the rising stars of the Al Nahyan dynasty, providing insight into their backgrounds, credentials, and positions within the complex family network.

Tradition and modernity coexist to shape the dynamics of leadership succession in the Al Nahyan family. The family values their heritage and ancestry, but they also understand that they need leaders who can skillfully lead them through the challenges of the modern world. An analysis of the leaders' educational and experiential backgrounds reveals a dedication to comprehensive preparation for the responsibilities associated with heading one of the world's most powerful families.

Evolving Investments and Strategies

The Al Nahyan family's next generation must reevaluate their investment strategies in light of the quickly shifting global environment. This section explores the changing investment strategies and approaches that the up-and-coming leaders have embraced.

Understanding how the family modifies its investment portfolio offers insight into their adaptability and foresight in light of market dynamics, geopolitical changes, and technological advancements.

With the next generation in charge, the Al Nahyan family's record-breaking success in managing sovereign wealth funds is probably going to take on new dimensions. The family's dedication to remaining at the forefront of economic trends is revealed by investigating possible changes in investment focus, areas of interest, and international partnerships. Additionally, learning about the family's resilience and inventiveness can be gained by looking at how they strike a balance between established and developing industries.

Opportunities and Difficulties

Taking charge of a family with such worldwide impact has its own set of opportunities and challenges. The challenges that the next generation is expected to face are examined in this section, and they range from economic fluctuations to geopolitical uncertainties. It looks at sustainable investing, technological advancements, and the possibility of further diversification all at the same time.

Under the leadership of the upcoming generation, the Al Nahyan family's global influence is expected to persist. The family's capacity to innovate, adapt, and preserve their legacy will be essential as they negotiate a complicated and interconnected world. An outlook on the family's lasting impact can be obtained by evaluating how they handle difficulties and take advantage of chances.

In summary, new leaders will emerge, investment strategies will change, and opportunities and challenges will need to be navigated by the Al Nahyan family. The world waits to see how this powerful dynasty will continue to influence the future of the world's landscape as the next generation assumes leadership.

Chapter 11. Conclusion

- Reflections on the Al Nahyan Legacy
- Lessons from the Pinnacle of Global Wealth

Reflections on the Al Nahyan Legacy

It is crucial to consider the significant legacy the Al Nahyan family has established over generations as we draw to a close our investigation of them. The Al Nahyan story is one of tenacity, foresight, and steadfast dedication to their people and the larger world—from modest Bedouin beginnings to becoming a worldwide force. This section explores the main tenets of the Al Nahyan legacy and how their history continues to influence their present and future.

The history of the United Arab Emirates (UAE) is closely linked to the Al Nahyan legacy. It is clear from thinking back on their voyage that their leadership was essential to the founding and advancement of the country. From Dhiyab bin Isa Al Nahyan to Sheikh Mohamed bin Zayed Al Nahyan, the present ruler, these visionary leaders have not only led Abu Dhabi through many momentous developments but have also played a crucial role in maintaining the emirates' unity.

The Al Nahyan heritage extends to economic strength in addition to political leadership. Their ability to grasp strategy is demonstrated by the creation and administration of sovereign wealth funds, such as the Abu Dhabi Investment Authority (ADIA) and Mubadala Investment Company. The family's contributions to the UAE's economic diversification have had a lasting impact, transforming the country from an oil-dependent economy into a multidimensional global participant.

Lessons from the Pinnacle of Global Wealth

Several themes emerge as guiding principles as we extract lessons from the Al Nahyan family's ascent to the top of global wealth. The careful balancing act between tradition and modernity is one of these lessons. With a forward-thinking outlook that embraces innovation, education, and technical breakthroughs, the Al Nahyan family has skillfully combined respect for their Bedouin history.

The family's dedication to the welfare of society is another important lesson. The charitable endeavors of the Al Nahyan family, especially in the fields of healthcare and education, are a prime example of their duty to improve not just their own community but also communities around the world. Recognizing that money, in the right hands, can drive great change emphasizes a more general mindset that goes beyond achieving financial success.

The Al Nahyan lineage also teaches us the importance of perseverance in the face of adversity. The family has demonstrated a remarkable capacity to withstand storms, from handling modern issues to navigating coups in its early years. Their adaptable thinking and tenacity make them an inspiration to other families managing the challenges of power and money.

To sum up, the Al Nahyan legacy is proof of the persistent value of foresight, initiative, and prudent financial management. Their tale has a universal resonance and is not just a part of UAE history. We acknowledge the Al Nahyan family not just as national leaders but also as the creators of a legacy that cuts beyond boundaries and generations as we learn from and are inspired by their journey.

Appendix

- Key Figures and Dates
- Glossary of Terms

Key Figures and Dates

1. The first of the Al Nahyan family's dynasties to rule Abu Dhabi was founded by Dhiyab bin Isa Al Nahyan (1761–1793).

2. Zayed bin Sultan Al Nahyan (1918-2004): First President of the United Arab Emirates from 1971 to 2004; visionary leader and founder of the country.

3. Khalifa bin Zayed Al Nahyan (1948–2022): The UAE's second president, in charge of the country's expansion and advancement from 2004 until his demise.

4. Present President of the United Arab Emirates, Mohamed bin Zayed Al Nahyan (1961–) carries on the family's tradition of leadership.

5. The Al Nahyan family is in charge of the Abu Dhabi Investment Authority (ADIA), one of the biggest sovereign wealth funds in the world, which was founded in 1976.

A Glossary of Terms

1. Bani Yas Tribe: A powerful tribal alliance on the Arabian Peninsula, of which the Al Nahyan family is a notable branch.

2. Sovereign Wealth Fund: A state-owned investment fund that is used to support the national economy and populace, and is frequently financed by profits from natural resources.

3. Al Bu Falah Dynasty: This was the first Al Nahyan dynasty to control Abu Dhabi, having been established by Dhiyab bin Isa Al Nahyan.

4. Trucial Oman Scouts: a British-led military unit in the United Arab Emirates that took part in the peaceful overthrow of Shakhbut bin Sultan Al Nahyan.

5. Sheikh Issa bin Zayed Scandal: 2009 controversy around Sheikh Issa bin Zayed's alleged torture of a man, which highlighted problems within the Al Nahyan family.

6. Mubadala Investment Company: A sovereign wealth fund that was founded in 2002 and adds to the United Arab Emirates' economic diversification.

The Abu Dhabi Investment Authority (ADIA) is a globally renowned sovereign wealth fund that oversees a varied array of international investments.

Printed in Great Britain
by Amazon